CONTENTS

GW00600677

© 1995 Burgundy Books, Hook, Hants, RG27 9BX.

No part of this publication may be reproduced in any form without the written permission of Burgundy Books.

ISBN 0 9526953 0 8.

Designed by the Royal Mail Design Studio, Swindon.

2 | **1 INTRODUCTION**

The information contained in this book is based on the author's 10-years' experience in the motor trade as salesman, business manager and sales manager.

The book contains a number of good ideas, any one of which could save you many times the cost of the book.

However, you will not save money by simply reading the book! It is the use of the information in the form of your preparation, action and persistence that will produce results!

Remember also that the majority of car dealers are hard-working businessmen, offering a good service to the public.

However, like any other businessmen, they have to make a profit to survive. The aim of this book is to enable you, the customer, to negotiate a deal that both you and the dealer can live with.

IMPORTANT! Since buying a car is a major purchase for most people, it is strongly recommended that you seek professional advice before entering into any financial commitment.

Finally, for the sake of clarity the term 'salesman' has been used to represent both men and women sales staff. No offence is intended to saleswomen!

Patrick Hoy.

October 1995

2 GET TO KNOW THE DEALERSHIP SYSTEM 3

CONTENTS   PAGE

4

THE MANUFACTURER/DEALER NETWORK

Did you know?

- When a dealer gets his stock of new cars he has a fixed period (usually 90 days) before he either has to pay for the cars or start paying interest charges.

- Some manufacturers supply cars on a build-to-order basis, eliminating the need to store new cars for long periods of time, prior to selling them.

- If a dealer does anything to damage a manufacturer's reputation, not only can he incur financial penalties, he can also lose his franchise!

Here's what you can do!

- Wait until the salesman has offered you a deal on the car of your choice, then ask how long it has been in stock. If it's been in the showroom for a while, try for a bigger discount. If the salesman won't budge, ask to look at a car that's been around longer. Keep on about the interest charges and if that doesn't work, go elsewhere!

- If you would prefer to buy a new car that has not been kept in storage, contact the Society of Motor Manufacturers and Traders (SMMT) and ask for a list of manufacturers who will build to order.

- If after you have taken delivery of your new car you have reasons to complain, but the dealer does not act in a fair and reasonable manner, tell him you will contact the manufacturer. If there have been other complaints the chances are the dealer may be at risk of losing financial incentives, so he might suddenly become very much more co-operative!

WHAT YOU NEED TO KNOW ABOUT CAR SALES STAFF

Did you know?

- Any presentable person, with good communication skills, the need to earn money, and a dominant personality, stands a good chance of getting a job in car sales.

- Very few salespeople are *trained* to sell cars; they just learn by trial and error!

- Typically, sales staff work 6 days a week (including Saturday and Sunday on a rota basis), from 8:30 am to 7:00 pm (plus a late night rota to 8:00).

- Basic salaries are around £5000 p.a. with an average commission of 10% of the profit retained after dealership charges have been deducted.

- Sales staff are under constant pressure to sell cars; if they don't, they may either not be able to live on their basic salaries, or they may risk losing their job.

- The retail motor trade has one of the highest rates of sales staff turnover, if not the highest!

Here's what you can do!

- Learn how to negotiate with sales staff by reading Sections 4, 5 and 6 of this book.

- Remember that their need to make a deal is probably greater than yours!

6   WHO'S WHO IN THE DEALERSHIP

Did you know?

A typical dealership staff 'tree' is as shown below. Each of the areas of responsibility indicated will affect you in some way, throughout the process of buying and taking delivery of your next car. Of course, dealership size varies, so that in some cases the same person may have responsibility for more than one of these roles.

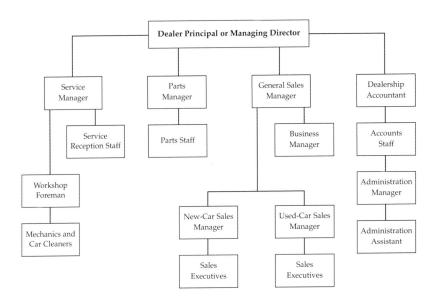

Here's what you can do!

- To get a good deal, get to know the right salespeople to talk to - and when.
- Find out who the Sales Manager is - he usually has to agree the deal.
- Remember that the Business Manager may try to sell you finance, but you don't have to buy it. If he is too persistent, complain to the Dealer Principal.
- Once you've bought the car, find out who the key people in other departments (e.g. Service) are - these are the people who are now most important to you.
- If at any stage of the process you are not satisfied with the deal you are getting, ask to see the Dealer Principal.

NEW-CAR PROFIT MARGINS (I)

Did you know?

- New-car profit margins usually come from several sources:

  - Straight percentage margin over wholesale, usually 5-10%.

  - Manufacturer's bonuses, from £50 to £1500 per car, depending on the make. If a salesman believes you are serious about buying a car, especially there and then, he will usually be prepared to openly discuss manufacturer's bonuses.

  - Manufacturer's rebates (around 1-3%) depending on the individual models/ranges and subject to the dealer meeting certain customer care and service targets.

  - Profits on the delivery pack and accessory sales.

  - Dealer finance.

Here's what you can do!

- Ask for a discount of around 7-8%. If the dealer wants to shift the car (see page 4) he may well cut his profits by this amount. If not, see how far he will go!

- Ask at the outset which vehicles are currently attracting the best manufacturer's bonus - you may get a good discount on any number of cars! But beware, the cars with the biggest discounts may not be those you need or can afford! Don't go over your budget just because a normally expensive car is cheaper than usual. With luck though, you may be able to get a car of a higher specification *without* exceeding your budget.

- Once you've agreed a discount on a car, ask for a discount on any factory-fitted items you order.

- Ask for a discount on the delivery pack - it could pay for your road tax or a tank of petrol.

8

NEW-CAR PROFIT MARGINS (II)

- If you need finance, don't agree to the dealer's proposition until you have looked at the alternatives (see page 12). Note that when cars have manufacturer-supported low-rate finance offered with them, the manufacturer's bonuses may be excluded. In this case you must decide between a low-rate finance offer or a heavily-discounted car (see Section 3).

Useful background information

i

The *delivery pack* is simply the cost from the manufacturer to the dealer for transportation of the car from the factory to the dealer's premises, the costs of preparing the vehicle for sale (often called the PDI), the supply and fitting of the number plates and the cleaning of the car prior to your collection. Delivery pack charges would usually be designed to carry a profit of around £50 to £100.

Accessory sales that are 'factory fitted' options usually have the same profit margin as the car itself (although in some cases the manufacturer's bonuses may be excluded). Therefore if you are buying an in-car CD Multi-play system at a retail cost of say £750 before VAT, a discount off retail of 7% would give you an extra saving of £61-68. Enough to buy some CDs to play on it!

A *manufacturer's bonus* is a payment, or series of payments, made to a dealer as an incentive to sell a particular model (or model range) that is either about to be superseded or of which there is a glut of stock. These bonuses may also be paid by manufacturers at times when the competition is most intense (for example, in August) as an incentive to dealers to sell their cars. A bonus may range from £50 per car up to £1500 on selected models.

USED-CAR PROFIT MARGINS

Did you know?

- The mark-up on a used car could be between £600 and £1500.

- If a dealer offers you wonderful giveaways, low- or zero-finance deals, or offers to pay your finance deposit, he has probably marked-up the price of the car substantially to cover his generosity (but read on…!).

- Dealers usually put a limit (30, 60, 90) on the number of days a used car should stay in stock before it is sold (they don't like money being tied up for long!). After a car has been in stock for a while, the dealer's desire to make a profit turns into a concern to recoup the amount paid for the car (plus costs) so that he can buy something else that may sell faster.

- Salespeople may be given a bonus for selling cars that are near the end of their stock period.

- A dealer may offer you an inflated value for your part-exchange, and then try to recover the difference in other ways, for example, on a finance deal.

Here's what you can do!

- Ask to see the cars that have been in stock for a while, or visit the showroom over several weeks and note which cars the dealer can't sell.

- Wait until the salesman has offered you a deal, then ask how long the car has been in stock. If it's been in the showroom for some time, try for a bigger discount. If the salesman won't budge, ask to look at a car that's been around longer. Keep on about the allotted number of stock days and the salesman's bonus, and if that doesn't work go elsewhere!

- Don't mention your part-exchange until *after* you've negotiated a deal. The salesman will then have to give you an accurate valuation of your old car.

3 HOW TO STACK THE DEAL IN YOUR FAVOUR

CONTENTS	PAGE

HOW ABOUT FOUR THOUSAND ONE POUND INSTALMENTS?

STAY WITHIN YOUR BUDGET

Did you know?

- Not knowing how much you can afford to spend before going into a showroom can put you in a weak negotiating position.

- If you know your limit, but don't stick to it, you may either buy a car you don't really need, or pay more than you need to for the car of your choice.

Here's what you can do!

- If you are using your savings:
  - *Before* looking at car prices, work out how much money you ought to keep for emergencies.
  - Work out the 'extras' such as insurance, road tax and running costs and deduct this to arrive at the amount you can afford.

- If you are borrowing the money:
  - Decide how much a month you can afford to repay (allow for increases in mortgage rate or rent).
  - Work out the 'extras' such as insurance, road tax and running costs.
  - Work out (see below) what your affordable monthly payment will buy you in the showroom. Ask at your bank, and phone a few dealers, to find out the best flat rate of interest available.
  - Choose a repayment period that's best for you (remember that a car is a depreciating asset!).

- Whichever way you intend to pay, remember to take into account the value of your old car (whether you intend to sell it privately, or offer it as part-exchange).

Useful background information

i

A flat rate of interest is the figure that exposes the total interest paid on a loan, e.g.:

$$\text{Flat rate } (\%) = \frac{100 \times \text{Interest}}{\text{Loan} \times \text{Period}}$$

For example, if you borrow £4000 over 3 years and pay £1080 interest, your flat rate is:

$$\frac{100 \times 1080}{4000 \times 3} = 9\%$$

12 | ## KEEP TO YOUR PREFERRED METHOD OF PAYMENT

Did you know?

- A salesman (or Business Manager) will do his best to sell you finance and insurance.

- If you don't stick to your payment plan, you may either buy a car you don't really need, or pay more than you need to for the car that you planned on.

- Knowing what you want, and sticking to it, helps you to stay in control of the negotiating process.

Here's what you can do!

- Before deciding which method of payment is best for you, study each option:

  - Paying by cash might earn a discount, but could you invest the money profitably elsewhere?

  - Borrowing from a bank, or building society, could be cheaper than dealer finance, but you might need that loan facility later on for an emergency.

  - A low finance rate from the dealer may disguise a higher than average price for a particular car.

- If you are unsure about dealer finance, ask a dealer to give you a complete breakdown of costs *and go away to think about it*. This will give you a chance to compare the 'bottom line' with other methods of payment (and, possibly, with offers made by other dealers).

Useful background information

Most dealer finance is HP, which means you don't own the car until all the payments are made, and it could be repossessed if you can't keep up the repayments.

Bank or building society loans tend to be personal loans which means that although you have a commitment to the lender, the car is yours from the start, and cannot be repossessed as with HP.

Dealer finance usually requires a deposit of at least 10% of the purchase price, whereas bank/building society loans do not usually require a deposit.

REMEMBER THAT THE APR IS IMPORTANT - BUT NOT VITAL   13

Did you know?

- In the motor trade, a low APR is not necessarily better for you than a high APR.

- Some dealers may deliberately attempt to steer you away from asking about the APR by focusing only on the monthly or weekly repayments.

Here's what you can do!

- If a dealer offers you a low APR, find out what deposit he wants. If you can't afford the deposit, you may have to accept a higher APR.

- Before agreeing to a finance deal, shop around and compare not only the APRs, but also the total amount of money that you will be paying back over the loan period.

Useful background information

Annual Percentage Rate (APR) represents the total charge for credit upon entering a loan agreement, including items such as documentation fees and option-to-purchase fees.

APRs are often used to compare different finance packages and different providers. However, things aren't always as simple as that, since other factors can influence the value of an APR, including the length of the agreement and when the interest element is repaid.

The deposit you have available is also important when comparing APRs. A deal based on 0% APR finance would immediately seem better than one offering 16.8% APR, until you find out the 0% deal requires you to have a deposit of 50% of the value of the car, whereas the 16.8% deal only requires 10%. If a 10% deposit is the best you can do, it is pointless looking at deals that require any more than that regardless of how low the APR may be!

14

Don't Be Fooled By A Great-Looking Repayment Plan

Did you know?

- Some dealers may offer an attractive-looking and unusual repayment plan, which is different from those offered by their competitors, so that you cannot easily compare plans, and thus choose the best deal for you.

- An attractive or unusual repayment plan may hide an unnecessarily high APR.

Here's what you can do!

- Don't reject a finance deal just because it is unusual, just make sure that you find out the total amount you have to repay, and the actual APR. Once you have this information you will be able to compare these two factors in all the finance deals on offer and make an informed decision.

Useful background information

Here are two examples of a repayment plan that might be offered - perhaps on the same car:

Details	Deal A	Deal B*
Cost:	£5,995.00	£5,995.00
Deposit:	£1,199.00 (20%)	£599.50 (10%)
Balance to finance:	£4,796.00	£5,395.50
Over period of:	36 months	45 months
At a repayment of:	£173.19 per month	£86.93 for 3 months
At a repayment of:	N/A	£0.00 for 3 months
At a repayment of:	N/A	£173.86 for 39 months
Flat Rate used:	10 per cent	12 per cent
Approximate APR:	19.6 per cent	23.6 per cent
Total charge for credit:	£1,438.84	£1,645.63
Total repaid:	£7,433.84	£7,640.63

* Deal B is advertised as:

'Only 10% deposit and £20.06 a week** - we pay half your repayments for 3 months and then there's nothing to pay for a further 3 months!'

** [this refers you to the small print, where you find the fully written credit example as required by law]

Deal B gives you a discount of £782.37 which you might find acceptable. Overall, however, deal B costs £206.79 more than deal A. What's more, having been offered a discount through the advertisement it is unlikely you will get any more, whilst deal A as it stands is still open to haggling!

Which deal do *you* think is best?

NEGOTIATE A DEAL - THEN SELL YOUR PART-EXCHANGE PRIVATELY 15

Did you know?

- Almost all part-exchange cars have a trade (wholesale) value as well as a retail value.

- If a dealer offers you a price for your part-exchange that is higher than its trade value, it will usually be at the expense of the equivalent amount of discount off the new car and/or finance arrangements.

- The AA and the RAC (and similar organisations) can give you a written report on your vehicle to show to prospective private purchasers.

- Organisations such as the Nationwide Used Car Arbitration Ltd (NUCA) can offer a private warranty scheme to give private purchasers more confidence in buying your car.

- If you can sell your old car privately at the full retail price, and get the maximum discount on your new car, you may do better than if you had part-exchanged your car with the dealer.

Here's what you can do!

- Check magazines (such as Exchange & Mart) and newspapers advertising used cars for sale, to find out the going retail price for cars similar to yours.

- Use the information in this book to negotiate with the dealer on the basis of no part-exchange, thus obtaining your discount as a reduction in the price of the new car and/or a discounted finance package.

- Use the organisations mentioned above and advertise your car privately.

- Don't make misleading claims about your vehicle.

- Don't hand over your car and its documentation until you have received cleared funds from the buyer.

Useful background information

Most publications that advertise used cars for sale offer advice on the do's and don'ts of selling a car privately.

Page 29 describes the way some dealers may try to undervalue your part-exchange.

Contact Burgundy Books if you would like more information about NUCA.

16

TAKE EXTRA PRECAUTIONS WHEN BUYING A USED CAR

Did you know?

- A car that has not been serviced to the manufacturer's specifications:
  - may forfeit any remaining warranty entitlements (which could mean big repair bills for you);
  - may be worth less because of its incomplete service history;
  - may have non-genuine replacement parts fitted.
- A car that has had more owners than the salesman tells you:
  - may have been a rental or lease-hire car (and therefore possibly heavily used);
  - will probably fetch less when you come to resell it.
- A car with outstanding finance on it, may not be legally yours until the outstanding finance has been cleared.
- A car that has been involved in a major accident, could have a serious structural defect.
- Not all dealers are able to guarantee the accuracy of the recorded mileage of their used cars.

Here's what you can do!

- Check the car's ownership history (e.g. number of owners, type of use).
- Make sure that the service record has been properly stamped and signed.
- Make sure that the details on the vehicle registration document match the car.
- Ask for written confirmation that the car is not subject to any finance agreement.
- Ask if a new odometer has been fitted - if it has, find out the mileage recorded on the old one (if you know the total mileage, you can estimate the total wear on the car). If possible, contact the previous owner to confirm the mileage.
- Ask for written confirmation that the car has not been involved in a major accident.

Useful background information

The best way to avoid the pitfalls described above is to go to a reputable dealer. However it is always advisable to know what questions to ask and what to look for when buying a used car.

4 UNDERSTAND THE DEALER'S SALES TECHNIQUES

CONTENTS   PAGE

18

WHO TAKES CONTROL - WINS!

Did you know?

- An experienced salesman will almost invariably try to take psychological control of the sales process right from the start. He may do this in a number of ways:

  - By talking to you on any subject but cars (e.g. the weather, the traffic, your family, last night's soccer results) so as to take your mind off the negotiating process.

  - By getting you to relax and place your trust in him.

  - By getting you to respond continuously to *his* statements and questions, thereby keeping you reactive instead of proactive.

  - By finding out what your *hidden* desires are.

- If you lose control of the sales process you may end up paying too much for a car that is not necessarily right for you.

Here's what you can do!

- Read the rest of this section and Section 5 *before* going to the showroom.

- Play the salesman at his own game by forcing him to respond to *your* questions.

- Ask the salesman how near he is to meeting his targets; which cars have been in stock the longest; which new cars are attracting the most manufacturer bonus etc., etc.

- If you feel that the situation is getting out of your control, politely make your excuses and leave - there is always another day and another showroom!

Useful background information

Even if you remain reactive throughout the whole process, you may still end up with a car that is right for you and meets your needs, basically because the salesman is content to strike a deal that is fair to both of you. However, by taking control of the negotiation you protect yourself against the unscrupulous salesman who wants to stack the deal in his favour.

NEVER BUY A CAR ON EMOTION ALONE

Did you know?

- A good salesman will try to make you fall in love with a car before revealing its true cost!

- Many people buy a car on emotion alone, without making sure that they can afford it!

Here's what you can do!

- Before you visit a dealer, work out the following:

    - What you *need* from a car, not just what you *want*.

    - What your motoring needs are likely to be in the future.

    - How much you can afford to spend (either in cash terms or in finance repayments).

    - What your running costs (e.g. insurance, road tax, petrol, repairs/servicing) are likely to be.

- Ask the salesman to show you cars that meet your specification, and get firm prices from him.

- Leave the showroom with this information and, at home, place the cars in order of priority, involving members of your family if you can.

- Work out the offer you are prepared to make and phone the salesman.

- If your offer is accepted, return to the showroom to test drive the car and complete your purchase.

- DO NOT exceed the financial budget you have decided on; if necessary, go to another dealer or rethink your choice of car.

20

HOW THE TRUE COST OF THE CAR CAN BE DISGUISED

Did you know?

- Car prices will usually vary quite considerably from dealer to dealer, even on the same model.

- Dealers will sometimes advertise/promote their cars in the form of finance repayments and/or special offer deals. This can make comparisons between dealers more difficult, and the cost of owning the car look more attractive.

- Negotiating solely on a finance repayment can result in little or no real discount being given.

Here's what you can do!

- Make sure you contact at least 3 or 4 dealers when buying your next car.

- No matter what type of deal is being offered to you, ask the salesman to either give you a vehicle price for a *cash sale* or details such as deposit, loan amount, flat rate of interest and total interest for a *finance deal*. You can then compare like with like at other dealers.

Useful background information

Fierce competition between dealers has resulted in them having to find ever more creative methods of making their cars attractive to buy. With more and more people needing either to use credit to finance their purchase or have their finance deposits paid for them, it can be easy to be overly impressed by a great-looking repayment plan (see page 14).

THE 'UP TO...DOWN TO' TECHNIQUE (I)

Did you know?

- Some salesmen believe a good deal is one where a customer has been persuaded:
  - To spend more than he intended, either as a cash price or as a finance payment.
  - To accept a lower price for his part-exchange than he had originally expected or asked for.
- One method used by such salesmen is called the 'Up To...Down To' technique.

Scenario 1: The Up To Ploy

Salesman: How much did you want to spend to get the right car, £3-400 per month or more?

(By starting high, the salesman draws the customer towards his maximum budget)

Customer: Not as much as that.

Salesman: Really, how far are we apart?

(This puts the onus on the customer, who will probably go higher than he intended!)

Customer: I was looking to spend about £180 per month.

Salesman: Up to a maximum of what?

(This usually unsettles the customer, who has to be pretty strong willed and sure of his negotiating position to insist that £180 *is* the maximum. He will usually go higher!)

Customer: Definitely no more than £190 per month.

(The £10 per month more the customer has just agreed to, using a 36-month term and an interest rate of 11% flat rate, has just given the salesman an extra £270.67 profit!)

Salesman: OK, but if I come across the right car for you that is just a few pounds over the £190, would you want me to exclude that?

(If the absolutely most perfectly matched car for you is available, and it is only £5 per month more, would you want to lose it?)

Customer: Well, no.

Salesman: I can understand how you feel. Shall we put an absolute limit of £195 on it?

Customer: Oh, alright then.

(By the way, the customer has just agreed to spend another £135.33!)

THE 'UP TO...DOWN TO' TECHNIQUE (II)

Scenario 2: The Down To Ploy

Salesman: That's a nice part-exchange you have there, how much were you looking to get for it, £2000, £2500, or less?

(Note that the salesman intentionally pitches this figure low, so as to take the customer as near to his minimum figure as possible)

Customer: I was looking to get £3500!

(Thinks 'But I could live with £3200')

Salesman: Down to a minimum of what?

Customer: I couldn't go lower than £3300.

Salesman: OK, but if in selecting the right car for you we have to go a little lower on your part-exchange, I guess you would probably want me to exclude that.

Customer: Not necessarily.

Salesman: I can understand that, you want to make sure you get the best car you can for your money. May I suggest that we put an absolute minimum of £3200 on it?

Customer: Er, I suppose so!

Here's what you can do!

- Take control of the negotiating process (see page 18).

- Turn the tables on the salesman by starting the conversation along the following lines:

  - "How much will you take for that car (showroom price £9000); £7500, £6500 or less...?"

  - "How much will you give me for my car (you want £3500); £4500, £5000 or more...?"

THE 'IF I CAN...WILL YOU?' MANAGEMENT REFERRAL PLOY   23

Did you know?

- Salesmen often want you to like the car *before* discussing the deal, so that you'll be less inclined to object when the full cost is revealed.

- Salesmen can put you under obligation, by implying that they are acting for you when they discuss the deal with their manager.

- By keeping you away from the decision-maker, a salesman can identify important details without having to agree to them himself.

Scenario (after a test drive)

Salesman:	I've told my manager that you want this car, and he has agreed to a price of £8995 on the road, with £2000 for your car.
Customer:	I want more than £2000!
Salesman:	That's understandable, but it seems a shame to lose this lovely car! How far apart are we on your part-exchange?
Customer:	Well, I was offered £2500 by another dealer only last week.
Salesman:	So if I can persuade my manager to give you £2500, do we have a deal?
Customer:	Yes. [salesman departs and returns later smiling]
Salesman:	I've told him that you really want this car and, since your car has a full service history, he's prepared to go to £2350. Is that OK?
Customer:	I really wanted £2500, can't you throw in the road fund licence?
Salesman:	If I can persuade him, will you sign an order now?
Customer:	Yes. [salesman goes off again and returns later with some documents]
Salesman:	Congratulations, I've persuaded him to throw in 6-months tax. When would you like to collect your new car?

Here's what you can do!

- Always discuss the deal *before* you get attached to the car.

- Ask to speak to someone who has the authority to agree a deal.

- Remember that the salesman may well be acting in his own interests, not yours!

24

5 BEWARE THE TRICKS OF THE TRADE

CONTENTS   PAGE

DON'T LET THE STRUCTURED SELLING SYSTEM GRIND YOU DOWN (I)

Did you know?

- A structured selling system is usually designed to:
  - identify your maximum budget (preferably in the form of a monthly repayment);
  - identify and/or build a desire in you to buy there and then;
  - persuade you to buy a car the dealer wants you to have.
- It usually works like this:
  - The salesman catches you before you have a chance to focus on a particular car (if you have an open mind, he has more chance of persuading you to buy the car he wants you to have).
  - He says:

    "To help me find the right car for you, may I ask you a few questions?"
  - If you agree, he asks you questions designed to identify your innermost buying tendencies (and takes control of the negotiating process!).
  - He suggests a car (or cars), and if you show interest, will persuade you to buy by identifying features and benefits that match those revealed by your answers (see next page).
  - Because the process is often lengthy and tiring, you agree to his suggestions.
- When it works, the structured sales process can generate substantial profits for the dealer.

Here's what you can do!

- Read Section 6 before going to the showroom.
- Ask the salesman if he is authorised to agree a deal with you. If he isn't, ask to speak to someone who is.
- Before the salesman starts, tell him politely:
  - What type of car you are after.
  - How much you want to spend.
  - The flat rate of interest and the period of repayment you want (if you want a finance deal).
  - What you want for your part-exchange (if applicable).

  This should restrict the salesman's ability to control the situation, and improve your chances of getting a good deal.

26 | ## DON'T LET THE STRUCTURED SELLING SYSTEM GRIND YOU DOWN (II)

Useful background information

i

Here's an example of the structured selling system:

Details	Car A	Car B
Make:	Ford	Ford
Model:	Escort 1.6LX	Escort 1.4LX
Colour:	Red	Blue
Reg No:	J123 XYZ	H131 ZYX
Days in stock:	10	50
Dealer wholesale price:	£5000	£4500
Dealer retail price:	£6395	£5895
Mileage:	36000	42000

You are looking for a low mileage Escort 1.6LX, and you spot Car A.

You have £1550 deposit and can afford repayments of around £175 per month (a borrowing power of £4846.15 assuming a flat rate of interest of 10% over a period of 36 months), so Car A is affordable.

However, Car B has been in stock longer than Car A and the dealer wants to shift it quickly. The sales controller therefore decides to try to interest you in Car B.

First, he calculates that he could push you to say £178 per month, at a flat rate of 12%, giving an APR of approximately 23.9%, and generating extra finance commission for the dealer.

This means you now have a borrowing power of £4711.76 over 36 months, and with your deposit of £1550, the controller has £6261.76 of your money to play with.

He then decides to build an extended warranty worth £300 on to the cost of Car B:

£(5895 + 300) - £1550 deposit = £4645 x 12% x 36 months = £175.48 p/m

Applying this to Car A:

£(6395 + 300) - £1550 deposit = £5145 x 12% x 36 months = £194.37 p/m

Since you think you can't afford Car A, you consider Car B. During the test drive, the controller will overcome all the objections you may have to the car, until you are left with no reason not to buy.

However, if you insist on Car A, and can stretch your budget to meet the increased monthly repayments, the controller will have made more profit on the deal than he expected, and can repeat the process with another customer.

Did you know?

- That a salesman may try to persuade you to buy a car by playing on your fear of 'losing out'.

Here is a popular routine used by salesman Dave and his colleague Andy. Picture yourself at Dave's desk. You have test driven the vehicle and looked at the figures. You know that this is the right car for you, yet something is holding you back.

Then Andy appears:

Andy: Sorry to interrupt, but I believe your customer has been looking at the red Mondeo?

Dave: That's right, we're just discussing the figures.

Andy: The problem is the chap who was in last night has just phoned, and he wants the car.

Dave: Has he left a deposit?

Andy: No, but he seems really keen!

Dave: When's he coming in?

Andy: As soon as I confirm that we've still got the car.

Dave: Can you give me a few minutes?

Andy: Okay, but hurry up, the manager's on my back...!

The question now is how badly do you want the car, because if you don't decide soon you'll lose it. Suddenly your doubts don't seem so important, because someone else is now seriously interested in the car *you* want so badly.

So, when the salesman (sensing your indecision) offers you a set of rubber floor mats or a tank full of petrol as a token acknowledgement to your bargaining position, it's hard not to succumb.

Here's what you can do!

- If there are important reasons for holding back, don't weaken! There will be other good cars.

- If you have already achieved what you wanted, and you are now haggling for the sake of it, *and* you really like the car, accept the situation and close the deal.

28

THE HARD MAN...SOFT MAN ROUTINE!

Did you know?

- That the salesman and sales manager may try to persuade you to accept their terms by pretending that one of them is bargaining with the other on your behalf.

- This well-rehearsed ploy usually occurs when you begin to show concern in the final stages of the negotiation.

Scenario 1: Hard Salesman - Soft Manager

You: I'm not sure about these figures, they seem too high!

Salesman: Well, we've gone as far as we can - you've got a really good deal there!

Manager: What's the problem - can I help?

Salesman: I was explaining that we've gone as far as we can on this deal!

Manager: I don't agree - I think we can adjust the figures down!

You are now more inclined to order the car because the manager has intervened on your behalf. Of course, the figures were set artificially high by the manager in the first place. Had you accepted them, the dealership would have made a windfall profit.

Scenario 2: Hard Manager - Soft Salesman

Salesman: I told my manager your absolute limit was £185 a month, but he wants £195!

You: I can't afford that!

Salesman: Well I'll tell him that it's £185 or nothing, but I'm definitely sticking my neck out!

Salesman: (Later) I've managed to get him down to £186.88, with a set of mud flaps thrown in!

You may be so grateful to the salesman that you don't have the heart to say that you wanted a deal that was under, not over, £185. But, had you agreed to £195, the dealership would have made even more profit.

Here's what you can do!

- Decide exactly how much you are prepared to pay, using the principles described in this book, and stick to it no matter what is said or who says it.

DON'T EXPECT TOO MUCH FOR YOUR PART-EXCHANGE!   29

Did you know?

- Much of a dealer's used-car stock comes from part-exchange deals.

- A major problem for the dealer is that he needs to sell you his car at *retail* price, and buy yours at *trade* price.

- A dealer will try to buy your car as cheaply as possible, to increase his profit margin.

- A dealer may distract you from the part-exchange price he is offering by:

  - claiming that since he has given you such a good deal on the car you are buying, he cannot possibly offer you as much for your part-exchange as you would like;

  - inflating the price of his used-car stock so as to be able to give apparently generous part-exchange allowances;

  - offering you a 'Trade for Trade' deal (see below);

  - being over-critical of your car, so as to mentally prepare you for a low evaluation.

Here's what you can do!

- Get part-exchange quotations from several dealerships.

- Ask several dealers how much they would give you for your car in a straight sale. This will strengthen your bargaining power when negotiating a part-exchange deal.

- If you are offered a Trade for Trade deal, ask if the manufacturer's bonuses have been included.

- If the deal seems too complicated, ask for a breakdown of costs.

- Consider selling your car privately (see page 15).

- Check out the various used-car price guides to get an idea of what your car is worth.

- Look at magazines/newspapers where used cars are advertised.

Useful background information

A Trade for Trade deal is where a dealer discounts the car he is selling you down to the manufacturer's wholesale price and then expects you to accept the lowest trade price for your part-exchange.

30

THINK TWICE BEFORE AGREEING TO A HOLDING DEPOSIT

Did you know?

- That asking for a holding deposit is usually the salesman's final attempt to get you to buy the car you're interested in, before you walk away from the showroom. His aim is to:

    - Make you feel that you may not be able to have that particular car unless you make your mind up there and then.

    - Give you a sense of commitment (and obligation) to the dealership.

    - Ensure that if you do decide to buy elsewhere you have to go back for your deposit, which gives him one last chance to change your mind.

Here's what you can do!

- If you are not completely sure that you want to go ahead with a deal, DO NOT agree to leave a holding deposit. The chances are that the car will still be there when you go back; if it isn't, there will always be others!

- If you should decide to leave a holding deposit, take the following precautions:

    - Get an official receipt; you will need this to get your money back.

    - Make sure the dealer writes on the vehicle order form "This order is subject to confirmation by (your name) on (specified date)", and signs underneath to acknowledge it.

Useful background information

 Some dealers may refuse to refund your deposit in an attempt to coerce you into buying the car. If this happens, make sure that you have your receipt and copy of the order form (as described above) and then complain to the Dealer Principal and/or your local Trading Standards Department.

6 DON'T BE AFRAID TO HAGGLE

CONTENTS   PAGE

32

YOU WON'T GET 10% OFF AT MARKS & SPENCER!

Did you know?

- People do not normally expect a discount off the purchase price of their goods:
  - When did you last insist on a 10% discount at Marks & Spencer?
  - Or negotiate a 5% discount on the fuel you buy to run your car?

- The motor trade is one of the few businesses in the UK where negotiating a discount is allowed, and indeed is the only way to secure a good deal for yourself.

- Car dealers expect customers to haggle, and have developed various strategies to counter people's attempts to negotiate a good deal.

- Some people think that if they get a good discount by haggling, they will be penalised afterwards, for example:
  - Their car will not be treated properly during the pre-delivery stage.
  - The dealer will not 'want to know' if things go wrong with their car.

Here's what you can do!

- Use this book to find out how car dealerships operate, and use this information to develop your negotiating skills.

- Don't take any notice if the salesman implies that your haggling is going against you in some way.

- Make sure that if you get a good deal by haggling, the details are confirmed in writing.

- If you feel that the dealer is not honouring the deal, complain first to the General Manager or Dealer Principal, and then to your Trading Standards Department or Citizens Advice Bureau.

Useful background information

If a dealer agrees to sell you a car for a price that you have negotiated then he is legally liable under various consumer protection laws for the condition and roadworthiness of the vehicle.

After you have taken delivery, the dealer is obliged to offer a minimum of three-months warranty, regardless of the price that the car was sold for.

DEALER PRICES ALLOW FOR HAGGLING

Did you know?

- Due to the intense competition that exists in the motor trade, there will always be some dealers who are prepared to undercut their competitors.

- The whole dealer pricing system is based on the principle that if some customers can be persuaded to pay top price, or are satisfied with a small discount, this will make up for the customers who negotiate a properly discounted deal.

- The dealer's final profit does not come from just one source; therefore what they lose on the price of the car may be made up in other ways.

- Dealer services offered to customers as part of the deal are priced on the assumption that a customer may have done his preparation thoroughly, so even if you have managed to haggle down the price of the car, you may lose out on the finance contract, warranty, accessories, etc.

- Since salesmen generally work on commission, customers who take up too much of their time negotiating discounts are not cost-effective.

Here's what you can do!

- Look carefully at each part of the overall deal package, determine what benefit you may derive from it and what you are willing to pay for it.

- Compare dealers on the deal element that is most important to you; for example, one dealer may charge slightly more for the car but give you a better finance deal.

- If negotiations are stalled, suggest that it is in the salesman's interest to close the deal and source another prospect.

Useful background information

The finance that is provided and arranged on your behalf is usually bought from the finance company for the equivalent of a wholesale price, and sold to you at a retail price. The same usually applies to extended warranties and credit insurance.

34

IF YOU ARE GOING TO HAGGLE - PLAN YOUR STRATEGY FIRST!

Did you know?

- Very few salespeople feel comfortable when asked directly for a discount (some may even give you more than you expected!).

- Salespeople don't like to haggle with someone who is well-informed and persistent.

- Very few customers make firm appointments to see salespeople.

- Salespeople do not usually like to discuss discounts over the telephone.

- Not knowing what you want before going into the showroom may allow the salespeople to take control and persuade you that comparisons with other dealerships are unnecessary.

Here's what you can do!

- Ask the salesman directly "How much discount will you give me?". If he says "How much do you want?", repeat the question. If he won't state a figure, go elsewhere!

- Keep accurate records of the dealers contacted and the discounts you have been offered.

- Always make a firm appointment with the salesman you want to see (if he thinks you are a serious prospect he is more likely to offer you a good deal!).

- Get all the information you can on list prices, special offers, finance rates, etc over the phone (then you won't be exposed to the dealer's sales technique until you are ready!).

- If a salesman won't give you information over the phone, politely remind him that if he doesn't, he stands no chance of getting your order. If this fails, go to the next dealer on your list.

Useful background information

 Planning your strategy away from the pressure of the showroom can improve your chances of negotiating a good deal. However, if nobody on your list of dealers will give you what you want, you could be aiming too high. Go home with the offers you have been given and think again!

ALWAYS ASK FOR A WRITTEN QUOTATION

Did you know?

- You may be given a verbal quotation which is low enough to undercut the competition, but too low for the dealer to honour.

- Having a written quotation improves your chances of getting a better deal elsewhere.

Here's what you can do!

- Negotiate a deal using the techniques described in this book and insist upon a written quotation. Take the written quotation to other dealers and ask them if they can do better. If they can't improve on the quotation, go back to the first dealer and finalise the deal (provided, of course, that the deal on offer is still the same).

- If the salesman won't give you a written quotation, write down the details and visit other dealerships to see if they can offer you a better deal (warning: other dealers may not be prepared to commit themselves if you don't have a written quotation!). If you can't get a better deal, go back to your first dealer. Be careful though, you might find that the deal you are ready to commit yourself to has mysteriously altered and is not quite as good as you thought it was.

This is what you might be told:

- "Sorry, I must have given you the wrong figures!"

- "Sorry, we must have been talking about different cars!"

- "Sorry, I didn't realise you wanted metallic paint!"

- "Sorry, you must have misheard me!"

Useful background information

If any part of your deal negotiation includes a finance quotation, a dealership is legally obliged to provide you with a written credit quotation. If a dealer will not do this, or is reluctant to do it, be very wary about the integrity of that dealer and, if necessary, inform your local Trading Standards Department.

36

If At First You Don't Succeed!

Did you know?

- Some dealers may try to defeat your attempts to haggle by:
  - not revealing which cars have the best discounts;
  - insisting that you fill in a customer appraisal form;
  - continually asking you questions and not answering yours;
  - ignoring, or rejecting, the plan you have worked out in advance;
  - being reluctant to give you specific credit repayment details.

Here's what you can do!

- First of all, don't panic if you cannot immediately apply the things you have learned from this book. You don't have to buy on your first or second visit to a dealership (or for that matter on your tenth). The most important factors in haggling are patience and persistence.

- If the sales staff won't answer your questions, explain that you are definitely going to buy a car but you need information to help you make a decision. Say firmly that you are prepared to sign an order there and then if they will answer your questions; if not, you will have to place your order elsewhere. Give them time to think about it, and if they still won't co-operate, go somewhere else.

- If a salesman tries to take control of the negotiation, or if you feel intimidated by his personality, ask to see someone else. Persevere with your plan, but if you feel that you cannot agree a deal, make an excuse and leave. Since it is possible that you are expecting too much, review your plan to see if it can be altered to satisfy both you and the dealer.

- If the Sales Manager or Business Manager won't give you specific details of their interest rates on finance deals, remind them of their legal obligations to provide you with a written credit quotation.

7 DON'T PAY MORE INTEREST THAN YOU HAVE TO

CONTENTS   **PAGE**

38

WHY THE DEALER WANTS TO SELL YOU FINANCE

Did you know?

- It has been estimated that some 70-80% of new and used cars are paid for with borrowed money.

- After expenses a dealership will normally retain about 70% of the commission generated by selling finance deals; this can amount to a third of the total profit generated from the sale of a car.

- To capitalise on this significant profit opportunity many dealers have trained specialist staff to actively promote and sell finance packages within the dealership (see page 39).

- It is in the dealer's interest to get you to buy a finance deal on the best terms he can get.

Here's what you can do!

- If you do not want dealer finance, say so at the outset and don't let anyone change your mind!

- If you decide that you want a finance package from the dealer, make them explain all the factors involved in the deal, particularly the rate of interest you will be paying.

- Shop around to get the best deal (get written quotations if you can).

Useful background information

Dealers usually act as brokers for finance companies and receive a commission on the amount and value (interest rate) of the business they generate. There are now many finance companies competing with each other, and many different finance packages available to the customer.

Even where low-rate deals are being offered to customers there is usually some kind of arrangement whereby the dealer obtains a commission relating not only to the interest rate sold, but also to the total amount of money lent through a particular brokerage arrangement per annum. This is often called a *volume bonus* and can be as high as 4% of the total amount of money that has been loaned to customers throughout the year.

BEWARE OF THE BUSINESS MANAGER

Did you know?

- The Business Manager earns commission from selling finance and related insurance. He usually has a persuasive and dominant personality and will try to get the highest rate of interest he can.

- He usually appears when you have agreed to buy a car, on the pretext of checking the order paperwork, explaining the vehicle warranty entitlement and arranging a date and time for collection.

- His real purpose however is to find out how you intend to pay for the car, and then persuade you by various means that you are making a mistake, for example:

  - *Bank loan?*   Borrow from us and keep your line of credit to the bank open!

  - *Cash?*   Borrow from us and keep your savings for 'a rainy day'!

  - *Another source of finance?*   Borrow from us and we'll beat their rate (whatever it is)!

Here's what you can do!

- Decide on your preferred method of payment in advance (see page 12).

- Try to gain control of the process (see page 18).

- If the Business Manager offers you a deal that looks attractive, don't change your plan there and then. Go home and think about it away from the pressure of the showroom!

Useful background information

There are usually two types of Business Manager: the traditional type who takes you through a separate sales process after you have agreed to have the car, and the progressive type whose target is to maximise commission from selling insurance (credit and mechanical breakdown) as well as finance. Progressive managers tend to work within a structured or controlled selling system as described on pages 25 and 26, and will get involved early on in the selling process. A good Business Manager of either type will aim to persuade 50-60% of customers to borrow money from him.

40   WATCH OUT FOR WEEKLY PAYMENTS!

Did you know?

- A dealer may suggest weekly payments because these appear more attractive than a lump sum:

  - Some people feel happier paying £34.10 a week than they do paying out £4000 at the start.

  - Some people would find the second offer below more attractive than the first:

    "I'll take your part-exchange and £4300 (not the £4000 you wanted - a difference of £300)."

    "I'll take your part-exchange and £35.83 a week (not the £33.33 a week you wanted - a difference of £2.50)."

- A dealer might suggest weekly payments to hide the true cost of the car or finance, for example:

  - You agree to pay £40 per week because you reckon you can afford £160 (£40 x 4) a month. It then comes as a shock when they want £173.33 a month (£40 times 52 weeks divided by 12).

- The use of weekly payments can also hide the true cost of accessories or credit insurance, etc.

Here's what you can do!

- Ask the salesman to give you the cash sum equivalent of weekly repayments on your car or finance. This will not only help you to decide if a deal is good value or not, but also allow a direct comparison with other dealers' quotations.

- Insist that repayment figures are quoted on a monthly basis (most repayments are paid monthly and are cheaper to collect than weekly repayments).

- When extras are being offered in return for a small additional payment amount per week, insist on knowing the true capital cost of the items.

Useful background information

The law states that a dealer may only advertise weekly repayments if he has the means to collect them weekly over the life of the finance agreement. It is worth checking to see if the dealer is complying with this ruling; if he is not, you may wish to rethink the repayment plan.

IF YOU WANT CREDIT INSURANCE - SHOP AROUND!

Did you know?

- Credit insurance is often sold on the emotional argument that by not spending just a few extra pounds per week you may be putting your family in jeopardy if for any reason (unemployment, sickness, etc.) you cannot keep up the repayments on your car.

- The Business Manager may offer you a very competitive rate of interest on finance, and then make it up by selling you credit insurance.

- A policy providing credit-protection cover in the event of redundancy, accident or illness can increase your monthly repayment by as much as 14%.

- The profit generated from the sale of credit insurance can range from 20% to 75% for the dealer and around 10-30% for the insurance provider.

Here's what you can do!

- Don't accept the dealer's credit-protection plan until you have looked at the alternatives offered by banks, building societies and other financial institutions - they may offer better value for money!

- Whichever plan you choose, always check the small print to see what is actually covered, for how much and for how long.

Useful background information

Many credit-insurance policies will only cover involuntary redundancy as opposed to unemployment; will only cover you if you have been in continuous employment (in the same company) for a period of 6 months prior to the commencement of the policy; will only start paying out after 14 or 30 days of the redundancy; and with regard to sickness or injury will have various exclusions such as disability due to back-related problems.

HOW TO CALCULATE THE OVERALL COST OF A CREDIT DEAL

Did you know?

- Many customers do not realise the total debt they are committed to when they sign a finance document.

- Many customers do not know the total amount that they are agreeing to repay, until they come to collect their car. It can therefore be very embarrassing to try to change or understand things at such a late stage, and of course there has been little opportunity to compare figures with other dealers or finance providers.

Here's what you can do!

Use the following headings to make sure that every credit deal that you are offered is split into its constituent parts so that you can make a comparison between individual items as well as the total amount:

		Example	*Your figures*	*Your figures*
1	On the road cost of the car:	£5995.00		
2	Deposit paid - cash:	£500.00		
3	Deposit paid - part-exchange:	£1650.00		
4	Balance of car to be financed 1-(2+3):	£3845.00		
5	Capital cost of any credit insurance:	£650.00		
6	Capital cost of any extended warranty or mechanical-breakdown insurance:	£295.00		
7	Capital cost of any accessories:	£0.00		
8	Other capital cost:	£0.00		
9	Total amount to be borrowed 4+5+6+7+8:	£4790.00		
10	Total monthly repayment:	£176.96		
11	Length of finance agreement (months):	36		
12	Proportion of monthly repayment relating to the car:	£142.05		
13	Proportion of monthly repayment relating to the credit insurance (if applicable):	£24.01		
14	Proportion of monthly repayment relating to the extended warranty or mechanical-breakdown insurance (if applicable):	£10.90		
15	Proportion of monthly repayment relating to any accessories (if applicable):	£0.00		
16	Proportion of monthly repayment relating to any other items (if applicable):	£0.00		
17	Total interest charge (10x11)-9:	£1580.56		
18	Documentation fee (if applicable):	£15.00		
19	Option to purchase fee (if applicable):	£25.00		
20	Total credit charge 17+18+19:	£1620.56		
21	Amount repayable over loan period (10x11)+18+19:	£6410.56		
22	**Amount repayable overall 1+5+6+7+8+20:**	**£8560.56**		

8 THE THINGS THAT CAN GO WRONG

CONTENTS   **PAGE**

44

When Your Car Is Not Ready On Time

Did you know?

- The *real* reasons for your car not being ready on time may be:
  - The cleaners haven't finished!
  - The keys are lost and there is no spare set!
  - The battery is flat!
  - The accessories you ordered are either wrong or have not been fitted!
  - The salesman never told anyone that he'd sold you the car!
  - Your car was accidentally damaged and the body repair shop are still working on it!
  - The wrong spare part was ordered and the mechanics are busy cannibalising another car!

- If the order form shows a specific date and time for you to collect the car, and if it has been signed by the salesman and the sales manager, then the dealership may be in breach of contract.

Here's what you can do!

- Telephone first - it may save you a wasted journey!

- If you know or suspect that unauthorised mechanical or bodywork repairs are being done, refuse to take delivery of the vehicle and demand your money back.

- If you suspect incompetence, complain to the management, explaining why and how you have been inconvenienced (for example, you might have taken time off work to collect the car).

- If you feel strongly enough, insist that they deliver the car to your home at a time that suits you. Alternatively, insist on compensation.

Useful background information

Most dealers will have your car ready on time and to the agreed specification. However, if problems arise due either to unforeseen circumstances or to dealership negligence, you must judge for yourself what action to take. If in doubt, contact your local Trading Standards Department.

Most reputable dealers belong to a trade association such as the Retail Motor Industry Federation and have a code of practice which protects you.

WHEN MULTI-PROPOSING AFFECTS YOUR CREDIT RATING   45

Did you know?

- When applying for credit from a dealer, your personal details may be offered to more than one finance company.

- Each time your details are put to a finance company, a 'search' is recorded against your name.

- If prospective lenders see a number of 'searches' recorded against you over a short period, they tend to think that you have applied and been refused elsewhere, and will probably refuse you themselves.

- If you leave your personal credit details with every dealership you visit, you may find that having decided on a car you want, your credit application is either declined or is subject to restrictive conditions such as an increased deposit, or a shorter repayment period.

Here's what you can do!

- Don't give your personal credit details to a dealer unless you have decided to buy a car from him.

- If you do give your credit details, ask the dealer to whom they will be proposing you, and why. If necessary, insist that your details are put to one company only, unless you say otherwise.

Useful background information

 If your application for credit is refused, you have a right to know why. Ask the finance company for details of the credit-reference agency that supplied information about you and your credit history, and write to them for a copy of all credit information they hold in your name at the addresses you have lived at for the previous seven years (there is usually a small fee for this!). If you disagree with what is on your file, you can appeal. Ask the credit-reference agency for details of the appeal procedure.

46 | **WHEN YOUR CAR DEVELOPS A FAULT**

Did you know?

- Although most new cars come with a 12-month parts and labour warranty as standard, some now offer a 3-year warranty as standard.

- Used-car warranties (or mechanical-breakdown insurance) tend to vary their cover depending on the age and make/model of the vehicle concerned.

- Some people do not think it is worth paying for mechanical-breakdown insurance on used cars.

Here's what you can do!

- Always get the best cover you can afford.

- Check the small print on warranties, particularly those on used cars, then weigh up the potential benefits against the cost.

- If you are not happy with the warranty offered to you by the dealer, try motoring organisations such as the AA and the RAC.

- If you can't afford a warranty, take precautions:

  - Use your test drive to expose any weak points the car may have (you need more than 20 minutes over the route selected by the dealer!).

  - If you can't spot mechanical faults - find someone who can (the AA or RAC will carry out an inspection, for a fee!).

- Finally, if you have no cover, go back to the dealer and ask him to look at the fault. If he values your custom (or your recommendation) he may do you a good deal on the repair!

Useful background information

Warranties/Mechanical-Breakdown Insurance Policies usually have the following stipulations:

- The amount the policy will pay per individual repair.

- The amount the policy will pay overall.

- The length of time your vehicle must be off the road before insurance repairs may start.

- The number of actual mechanical and electrical components that are covered by the policy.

- The amount payable to compensate you for any inconvenience suffered (for example, loss of transport, or a spoilt holiday).

WHEN YOU CAN'T AFFORD THE REPAYMENTS

Did you know?

- After buying a car, some people cannot afford the repayments, and need to trade down.

- Trading down too soon after buying can be expensive:

  Let's say an Escort 1.6L costing £5495 (£550 deposit and £178.56 a month for 36 months), is the right car for you.

  However, you see a lovely XR3i costing £6995 (deposit £700 and £227.32 a month over 36 months), and you buy it.

  Four months later your mortgage goes up £70 per month and you need to trade down.

  You owe £6050 on finance, and your Escort is worth £5200.

  You have £250 for a deposit, and the salesman offers you an inflated value for your car (£5500).

  You can afford £178 per month, so you can borrow £4950 (36 months at 10% per annum), but you need £550 deposit.

  To settle the finance contract, and give you £300 towards your deposit, the salesman increases the part-exchange allowance to £6350.

  He has now over-allowed on the part-exchange by £1150 (£6350 minus £5200) and must recoup this (plus a profit of say £500), giving a total of £1895 (inc VAT).

  Therefore he offers you a car that cost him £3605 (a Fiesta 1.1L, say).

  You'll be paying well over the odds for this, with little chance of changing it until the three-year contract has ended (assuming that the finance company accept you!).

  You also know that had you bought the Escort in the first place, you would have had a better car for the same price.

Here's what you can do!

- Know the difference between what you want, what you need, and what you can afford, **and always allow for changes in your circumstances!**

- If you act before the finance company has paid the dealer for the car, you may be able to unravel your deal and start again. Contact the finance company directly if necessary - **but act quickly!**

9 CHECKLIST

Have you

- worked out what you can *afford*?

- worked out the type of car you *need*?

- worked out how you are going to *pay*?

- decided what to do about your *part-exchange*?

Do you

- understand the *dealership system*?

- know how to reduce the *interest* you pay on finance?

- know how to work out the cost of a *credit deal*?

- know what to do if *things go wrong*?

Are you

- familiar with the *dealer's sales techniques*?

- familiar with the *'tricks of the trade'*?

- ready to *stack the deal* in your favour?

- ready to *haggle*?